HOW TO STUDY & KNOW THE BIBLE

(WITH A ONE-YEAR BIBLE READING PLAN)

Published by:

KARIS PUBLISHING

Website: www.karisconsult.com

Email: info@karisconsult.com

Unless otherwise stated, all scriptural references are taken from the New King James Version of the Holy Bible

Printed in Nigeria by:
SOS Publications
SOSPublications@yahoo.com
SOSPublications.com.ng

TABLE OF CONTENT

INTRODUCTION

This booklet is prepared to assist Christians to better appreciate the critical place of the Word of God, and its immense power and potential for constant victory in Christian warfare.

As I move around in ministry, I am amazed and dumbfounded to realize that most Christians are largely ignorant of God's Word. Even common passages that used to be at the fingertips of the average Christian few decades ago are now completely strange to most people who profess to be Christians today.

The ignorance of God's Word by Christians accounts in large measure for the falling away of the church, the spiritual weakness and defeat of many believers, the emergence of the age of godfatherism and personality worship, and why many Christians fall victim of false doctrines and fallacious teachings.

Getting a copy of the Bible is not the problem. God has made the Bible so cheap that N500 can fetch one a copy of the Bible, which even a student can afford. The key problem, as I see it, is that many Christians don't know the value and power of the Bible, and the fact that the whole of their lives depend upon it. The Word of God in the Bible will give you knowledge, discernment, wisdom, salvation, healing, protection, faith, power, holiness, healing, prosperity, financial breakthrough, favour, honour, glory, peace, joy, happy family life and good human relationships. Apart from not knowing the power and value of the Word of God, which is the primary problem, this primary problem is complemented and complicated by other secondary challenges such as worldliness, busyness, indiscipline, poor time management, and frustration and discouragement when many people come across passages that appear dry or difficult.

This book will help you to have a better appreciation of the power of the Word of God and why it must occupy a central place in your life. It also addresses the Frequently Asked Questions on personal Bible Study.

We also present a One-Year Bible Reading Plan, to assist you in a systematic and comprehensive study of the Bible, by which you are able to read the Bible from cover to cover in one year. We found the Website: ***eword.com*** quite helpful in preparing the One-Year Bible Reading Plan.

Finally, we outline some Bible passages that every serious and committed Christian must know by heart, as it used to be in the Church of few decades ago.

We trust that with discipline, prayer and determination, this book will turn your spiritual life around for good, in Jesus Name.

CHAPTER ONE

WHY YOU MUST KNOW THE BIBLE

The Word of God in End-Time Warfare

A sound knowledge of the Word of God is most central and highly imperative for constant victory in this end time battle. God, in His great love and mercy has given us His mighty Word as a spiritual weapon for pleasing Him and for defeating the devil and all his antics.

The Word of God is not just letter; it is spirit, it is life. It is compared to various weapons of warfare, like hammer, fire, and sword. The Word of God is food for the spirit, and potent instrument for the renewal of the mind. It is water that cleanses and purifies.

It is a sure way of overcoming and silencing the devil when he comes to tempt or attack us.

What will the Word of God do in your life?

The Word of God must be at the centre of the life of every believer because it has so much to do in your life; in fact, it is your very life (Deut.32:46-47; Jn.6:63).

i. A sound knowledge of God's Word will help you to know the perfect will of God for all situations. It reveals the will, mind, commandments and standard of righteousness of the Lord. It will help you to live a holy life and keep your heart pure. Sadly enough, many Christians and even ministers of the gospel have neglected the Word of God today and set up their own standard of righteousness. As you live by the Word of God, you are able to make your way and your life holy and pure.

ii. A good knowledge of the Word of God will keep you in sound doctrine, help you to know the authoritative truth of God and the things that are most important to God (love, faith and righteousness), and will save you from false doctrines, errors, lopsided emphasis, and majoring in minor, which is the plague of the church today.

iii. The Word of God will strengthen you in your inner man. It will make you strong to defeat the devil in all aspects of spiritual warfare. If you have a sound knowledge of the Word of God, it will be impossible for the devil to confuse and take advantage of you.

iv. The Word of God will make your faith strong; it is the only source of faith for the believer.

v. The Word of God will give you divine wisdom, the wisdom of God. Indeed, the Word of God is the wisdom and power of God, to which the devil and the world have no answer. Take note that the wisdom of God is totally different from the wisdom of this world. The wisdom of this world, though it may produce temporary result and an apparent victory, it eventually promotes ungodliness and leads to sorrow, death and destruction. The Wisdom of God, which often involves patience, humility, faith and righteousness, leads to life, lasting joy and complete victory, both in time and in eternity.

vi. A deep and sound knowledge of the Word of God will save you from hero worship, which is the bane of the church today. You will get to know God as your own Father, who has no grandchildren, who has a direct Father-Child relationship with all His children. The laziness of believers today in knowing God's Word from Genesis to Revelation is the main explanation for the way many 'Fathers in the Lord' are holding millions of souls captive, preventing them from knowing, receiving and living in the total truth of God, making them to see only what they want them to see. No wonder our Lord said that learning at His feet and knowing Him directly is that good part which Mary found, and which could not be taken away from her, or from any person that finds this secret (Lk.10:41-42).

vii. The Word of God provides you with the awesome promises of God which, when you stand upon them and firmly appropriate them, will lead you to victory over life challenges and over sin.

It is most sad and painful that Christians neglect the Word of God; they are too slothful and too unwise to devote much time to the Word of God, which God has freely made available to us all, and yet they want to have constant victory, which is absolutely impossible without a deep and sound knowledge of the Word.

How does God expect us to relate with His Word? What should be our right attitude to the Word of God, if we are serious about being victorious in end-time warfare and in the issue of living a holy life and making heaven?

We must read the Word of God every day – literally every day. It is the food of the soul and spirit. In the physical, the food eaten today cannot carry you for tomorrow, except you are fasting, and you are not expected to 'fast' in the Word of God. In the same way, the scripture you read yesterday cannot carry you for the warfare, temptations and challenges of today. You must renew your mind and feed your spirit with the Word of God every day. But only those who are determined to make heaven by all means will take this seriously and obey.

You must know every part of the Bible from Genesis to Revelation. You must know every book of the Bible in and out, if you want to know the truth, please God and make heaven. That means you must be systematic in your study of the Bible. As a young convert, you may achieve this goal of systematic study of the Bible by using a good daily devotional, like Daily Bread, Everyday with Jesus, Daily Manna, Open Heavens, and so on. But this is only okay for young converts. As you grow in the Lord, and you become some 4 to 5 years old in the Lord, the use of Daily Devotional alone is not enough. You must start reading the Books of the Bible one by one, from Genesis to Revelation, marking the verses with which the Holy Spirit ministers to you, taking down notes, until you finish the whole Bible. When you finish, you start all over again, because the mystery of this great Book is that the Holy Spirit keeps showing you new things in it every day. The volume of its truths, revelations, mysteries and power is simply infinite.

A book by book reading of the Bible does not stop you from moving to other parts of the Bible for some references or to specifically study some truths at any point in time, but as soon as you finish that one-off study or reference, you must go back to where you stopped yesterday. Don't skip scriptures that appear boring (Really no part of God's Word is boring; it's only apparently boring to you now because of your current spiritual state, or because God puts it there for a purpose that does not appear to concern you for now). You can read such parts of scriptures with speed without skipping them, while you can take some time later in the day to feed and nourish your spirit from your favourite passages of the Bible like in the Psalms or in the New Testament. But continue with your consistent study of the Bible book by book until you finish the Bible. You may also decide to read 2 books at the same time, one in the Old Testament and the other in the New Testament, until you finish the whole Bible. Through a systematic study of the Bible, you will finish the whole Bible in one to two years, and you start all over again.

You cannot afford to read the Bible as you read any secular book. You must think and meditate deeply on the verses of scriptures you are reading, because it carries a special message from God to you. It is a love letter from God to you, which is intended to convey and minister a blessing to you – to assure you, to correct you, to warn you, to impact a nugget of wisdom and light to you or to guide you in life decisions. Merely reading the Word of God without deep thinking and meditation is of little or no value. God does not ask us to merely read His Word, but to study and meditate on it, day and night.

You are also required to memorize the Word of God, to hide it in your heart. This occurs either through a conscious effort, or as you read a powerful and nourishing passage of Scriptures over and over again. I've found out from my own personal experience that most of the Scriptures I know by heart today become stamped in my heart because I have literally and cumulatively spent scores of hours ruminating, digesting, meditating, loving, and beholding the wonders of such passages, such that they become stamped on my heart indelibly, almost effortlessly. Only the Word of God that is hidden in your heart can avail for you and give you victory when challenges and temptations come, or when you require to attend to particular needs.

If you find the Word of God dry and uninteresting, you have to ask yourself if you are truly born again. If you are sure you are, then you must be filled and baptized with the power of the Holy Spirit, for it is the Holy Spirit alone that teaches us the Word of God, as He is the Author. Having been filled with the Holy Spirit, you should pray earnestly that God should open your eyes to behold wondrous things from His Word and that He should give you the spirit of wisdom and revelation knowledge in His Word, that the eyes of your understanding should be enlightened by His Holy Spirit that dwells in you.

Finally and most importantly, you must firmly believe the whole word of God with the determination to live by it, appropriate it and obey it completely, not selectively. If a person picks certain verses of Scriptures only because they present the promises of God to His children or enlighten us of our authority and position in Christ, but ignores or pays scant attention to its commandments, precepts and warnings, or disregards the abundant truths about heaven, hell, holiness and the nature of God's eternal Kingdom, such a person is unwise, majoring in minor and does not seriously desire and determine to make heaven. When you listen to the DVD messages from the servants of God sent to us in these last days, it will strike you that God is going to judge us by His Word and the devil is going to accuse man by the Word of God. Any verse from Genesis to Revelation can be referred to in judgment. It is therefore wise to pay close attention to the complete Word of God, standing on its promises, obeying its commandments and living by the wisdom and power of its revelations. This is the only way to achieve comprehensive victory and make heaven.

SECTION TWO

ONE-YEAR BIBLE READING PLAN

(With Discipline and Dedication, this Plan will help you to complete reading the Bible from Genesis to Revelation in One Year. A column is provided for you to tick, as you complete your reading of the Chapters for each day. We found the Website: eword.com quite helpful in preparing the One Year Bible Reading Plan)

JANUARY

DAY	**OLD TESTAMENT**	**NEW TESTAMENT**	TICK (✔) After Reading For Each Day
JANUARY 1	Gen 1-3	Matt 1	
JANUARY 2	Gen 4-6	Matt 2	
JANUARY 3	Gen 7-9	Matt 3	
JANUARY 4	Gen 10-12	Matt 4	
JANUARY 5	Gen 13-15	Matt 5:1-26	
JANUARY 6	Gen 16-17	Matt 5:27-48	
JANUARY 7	Gen 18-19	Matt 6:1-18	
JANUARY 8	Gen 20-22	Matt 6:19-34	
JANUARY 9	Gen 23-24	Matt 7	
JANUARY 10	Gen 25-26	Matt 8:1-17	
JANUARY 11	Gen 27-28	Matt 8:18-34	
JANUARY 12	Gen 29-30	Matt 9:1-17	
JANUARY 13	Gen 31-32	Matt 9:18-38	
JANUARY 14	Gen 33-35	Matt 10:1-20	
JANUARY 15	Gen 36-38	Matt 10:21-42	
JANUARY 16	Gen 39-40	Matt 11	
JANUARY 17	Gen 41-42	Matt 12:1-23	
JANUARY 18	Gen 43-45	Matt 12:24-50	
JANUARY 19	Gen 46-48	Matt 13:1-30	
JANUARY 20	Gen 49-50	Matt 13:31-58	
JANUARY 21	Ex 1-3	Matt 14:1-21	
JANUARY 22	Ex 4-6	Matt 14:22-36	
JANUARY 23	Ex 7-8	Matt 15:1-20	
JANUARY 24	Ex 9-11	Matt 15:21-39	
JANUARY 25	Ex 12-13	Matt 16	
JANUARY 26	Ex 14-15	Matt 17	
JANUARY 27	Ex 16-18	Matt 18:1-20	
JANUARY 28	Ex 19-20	Matt 18:21-35	
JANUARY 29	Ex 21-22	Matt 19	
JANUARY 30	Ex 23-24	Matt 20:1-16	
JANUARY 31	Ex 25-26	Matt 20:17-34	

FEBRUARY

DAY	OLD TESTAMENT	NEW TESTAMENT	TICK (✔) After Reading For Each Day
FEBRUARY 1	Ex 27-28	Matt 21:1-22	
FEBRUARY 2	Ex 29-30	Matt 21:23-46	
FEBRUARY 3	Ex 31-33	Matt 22: 1-22	
FEBRUARY 4	Ex 34-35	Matt 22:23-46	
FEBRUARY 5	Ex 36-38	Matt 23:1-22	
FEBRUARY 6	Ex 39-40	Matt 23:23-39	
FEBRUARY 7	Lev 1-3	Matt 24:1-28	
FEBRUARY 8	Lev 4-5	Matt 24:29-51	
FEBRUARY 9	Lev 6-7	Matt 25:1-30	
FEBRUARY 10	Lev 8-10	Matt 25:31-46	
FEBRUARY 11	Lev 11-12	Matt 26:1-25	
FEBRUARY 12	Lev 13	Matt 26:26-50	
FEBRUARY 13	Lev 14	Matt 26:51-75	
FEBRUARY 14	Lev 15-16	Matt 27:1-26	
FEBRUARY 15	Lev 17-18	Matt 27:27-50	
FEBRUARY 16	Lev 19-20	Matt 27:51-66	
FEBRUARY 17	Lev 21-22	Matt 28	
FEBRUARY 18	Lev 23-24	Mark 1:1-22	
FEBRUARY 19	Lev 25	Mark 1:23-45	
FEBRUARY 20	Lev 26-27	Mark 2	
FEBRUARY 21	Num 1-2	Mark 3:1-19	
FEBRUARY 22	Num 3-4	Mark 3:20-35	
FEBRUARY 23	Num 5-6	Mark 4:1-20	
FEBRUARY 24	Num 7-8	Mark 4:21-41	
FEBRUARY 25	Num 9-11	Mark 5:1-20	
FEBRUARY 26	Num 12-14	Mark 5:21-43	
FEBRUARY 27	Num 15-16	Mark 6:1-29	
FEBRUARY 28/29	Num 17-19	Mark 6:30-56	

MARCH

DAY	OLD TESTAMENT	NEW TESTAMENT	TICK (✔) After Reading For Each Day
MARCH 1	Num 20-22	Mark 7:1-13	
MARCH 2	Num 23-25	Mark 7:14-37	
MARCH 3	Num 26-28	Mark 8	
MARCH 4	Num 29-31	Mark 9:1-29	
MARCH 5	Num 32-34	Mark 9:30-50	
MARCH 6	Num 35-36	Mark 10:1-31	
MARCH 7	Deut 1-3	Mark 10:32-52	
MARCH 8	Deut 4-6	Mark 11:1-18	
MARCH 9	Deut 7-9	Mark 11:19-33	
MARCH 10	Deut 10-12	Mark 12:1-27	
MARCH 11	Deut 13-15	Mark 12:28-44	
MARCH 12	Deut 16-18	Mark 13:1-20	
MARCH 13	Deut 19-21	Mark 13:21-37	
MARCH 14	Deut 22-24	Mark 14:1-26	
MARCH 15	Deut 25-27	Mark 14:27-53	
MARCH 16	Deut 28-29	Mark 14:54-72	
MARCH 17	Deut 30-31	Mark 15:1-25	
MARCH 18	Deut 32-34	Mark 15:26-47	
MARCH 19	Josh 1-3	Mark 16	
MARCH 20	Josh 1-3	Luke 1:1-20	
MARCH 21	Josh 7-9	Luke 1:21-38	
MARCH 22	Josh 10-12	Luke 1:39-56	
MARCH 23	Josh 13-15	Luke 1:57-80	
MARCH 24	Josh 16-18	Luke 2:1-24	
MARCH 25	Josh 19-21	Luke 2:25-52	
MARCH 26	Josh 22-24	Luke 3	
MARCH 27	Jud 1-3	Luke 4:1-30	
MARCH 28	Jud 4-6	Luke 4:31-44	
MARCH 29	Jud 7-8	Luke 5:1-16	
MARCH 30	Jud 9-10	Luke 5:17-39	
MARCH 31	Jud 11-12	Luke 6:1-26	

APRIL

DAY	OLD TESTAMENT	NEW TESTAMENT	TICK (✔) After Reading For Each Day
APRIL 1	Jud 13-15	Luke 6:27-49	
APRIL 2	Jud 16-18	Luke 6:27-49	
APRIL 3	Jud 19-21	Luke 7:31-50	
APRIL 4	Ruth 1-4	Luke 8:1-25	
APRIL 5	1Sam 1-3	Luke 8:26-56	
APRIL 6	1Sam 4-6	Luke 9:1-17	
APRIL 7	1Sam 7-9	Luke 9:18-36	
APRIL 8	1Sam 10-12	Luke 9:37-62	
APRIL 9	1Sam 13-14	Luke 10:1-24	
APRIL 10	1Sam 15-16	Luke 10:25-42	
APRIL 11	1Sam 17-18	Luke 11:1-28	
APRIL 12	1Sam 19-21	Luke 11:29-54	
APRIL 13	1Sam 22-24	Luke 12:1-31	
APRIL 14	1Sam 25-26	Luke 12:32-59	
APRIL 15	1Sam 27-29	Luke 13:1-22	
APRIL 16	1Sam 30-31	Luke 13:23-35	
APRIL 17	2Sam 1-2	Luke 14:1-24	
APRIL 18	2Sam 3-5	Luke 14:25-35	
APRIL 19	2Sam 6-8	Luke 15:1-10	
APRIL 20	2Sam 9-11	Luke 15:11-32	
APRIL 21	2Sam 12-13	Luke 16	
APRIL 22	2Sam 14-15	Luke 17:1-19	
APRIL 23	2Sam 16-18	Luke 17:20-37	
APRIL 24	2Sam 19-20	Luke 18:1-23	
APRIL 25	2Sam 21-22	Luke 18:24-43	
APRIL 26	2Sam 23-24	Luke 19:1-27	
APRIL 27	1King 1-2	Luke 19:28-48	
APRIL 28	1King 3-5	Luke 20:1-26	
APRIL 29	1King 6-7	Luke 20:27-47	
APRIL 30	1King 8-9	Luke 21:1-19	

MAY

DAY	OLD TESTAMENT	NEW TESTAMENT	TICK (✔) After Reading For Each Day
MAY 1	1King 10-11	Luke 21:20-38	
MAY 2	1King 12-13	Luke 22:1-30	
MAY 3	1King 14-15	Luke 22:31-46	
MAY 4	1King 16-18	Luke 22:47-71	
MAY 5	1King 19-20	Luke 23:1-25	
MAY 6	1King 21-22	Luke 23:26-56	
MAY 7	2King 1-3	Luke 24:1-35	
MAY 8	2King 4-6	Luke 24:36-53	
MAY 9	2King 7-9	John 1:1-28	
MAY 10	2King 10-12	John 1:29-51	
MAY 11	2King 13-14	John 2	
MAY 12	2King 15-16	John 3:1-18	
MAY 13	2King 17-18	John 3:19-36	
MAY 14	2King 19-21	John 4:1-30	
MAY 15	2King 22-23	John 4:31-54	
MAY 16	2King 24-25	John 5:1-24	
MAY 17	1Chron 1-3	John 5:25-47	
MAY 18	1Chron 4-6	John 6:1-21	
MAY 19	1Chron 7-9	John 6:22-44	
MAY 20	1Chron 10-12	John 6:45-71	
MAY 21	1Chron 13-15	John 7:1-27	
MAY 22	1Chron 16-18	John 7:28-53	
MAY 23	1Chron 19-21	John 8:1-27	
MAY 24	1Chron 22-24	John 8:28-59	
MAY 25	1Chron 25-27	John 9:1-23	
MAY 26	1Chron 28-29	John 9:24-41	
MAY 27	2Chron 1-3	John 10:1-23	
MAY 28	2Chron 4-6	John 10:24-42	
MAY 29	2Chron 7-9	John 11:1-29	
MAY 30	2Chron 10-12	John 11:30-57	
MAY 31	2Chron 13-14	John 12:1-26	

JUNE

DAY	OLD TESTAMENT	NEW TESTAMENT	TICK (✔) After Reading For Each Day
JUNE 1	2Chron 15-16	John 12:27-50	
JUNE 2	2Chron 17-18	John 13:1-20	
JUNE 3	2Chron 19-20	John 13:21-38	
JUNE 4	2Chron 21-22	John 14	
JUNE 5	2Chron 23-24	John 15	
JUNE 6	2Chron 25-27	John 16	
JUNE 7	2Chron 28-29	John 17	
JUNE 8	2Chron 30-31	John 18:1-18	
JUNE 9	2Chron 32-33	John 18:19-40	
JUNE 10	2Chron 34-36	John 19:1-22	
JUNE 11	Ezra 1-2	John 19:23-42	
JUNE 12	Ezra 3-5	John 20	
JUNE 13	Ezra 6-8	John 21	
JUNE 14	Ezra 9-10	Acts 1	
JUNE 15	Nehemiah 1-3	Acts 2:1-21	
JUNE 16	Nehemiah 4-6	Acts 2:22-47	
JUNE 17	Nehemiah 7-9	Acts 3	
JUNE 18	Nehemiah 10-11	Acts 4:1-22	
JUNE 19	Nehemiah 12-13	Acts 4:23-37	
JUNE 20	Esther 1-2	Acts 5:1-21	
JUNE 21	Esther 3-5	Acts 5:22-42	
JUNE 22	Esther 6-8	Acts 6	
JUNE 23	Esther 9-10	Acts 7:1-21	
JUNE 24	Job 1-2	Acts 7:22-43	
JUNE 25	Job 3-4	Acts 7:44-60	
JUNE 26	Job 5-7	Acts 8:1-25	
JUNE 27	Job 8-10	Acts 8:26-40	
JUNE 28	Job 11-13	Acts 9:1-21	
JUNE 29	Job 14-16	Acts 9:22-43	
JUNE 30	Job 17-19	Acts 10:1-23	

JULY

DAY	OLD TESTAMENT	NEW TESTAMENT	TICK (✔) After Reading For Each Day
JULY 1	Job 20-21	Acts 10:24-48	
JULY 2	Job 22-24	Acts 11	
JULY 3	Job 25-27	Acts 12	
JULY 4	Job 28-29	Acts 13:1-25	
JULY 5	Job 30-31	Acts 13:26-52	
JULY 6	Job 32-33	Acts 14	
JULY 7	Job 34-35	Acts 15:1-21	
JULY 8	Job 36-37	Acts 15:22-41	
JULY 9	Job 38-40	Acts 16:1-21	
JULY 10	Job 41-42	Acts 16:22-40	
JULY 11	Ps 1-3	Acts 17:1-15	
JULY 12	Ps 4-6	Acts 17:16-34	
JULY 13	Ps 7-9	Acts 18	
JULY 14	Ps 10-12	Acts 19:1-20	
JULY 15	Ps 13-15	Acts 19:21-41	
JULY 16	Ps 16-17	Acts 20:1-16	
JULY 17	Ps 18-19	Acts 20:17-38	
JULY 18	Ps 20-22	Acts 21:1-17	
JULY 19	Ps 23-25	Acts 21:18-40	
JULY 20	Ps 26-28	Acts 22	
JULY 21	Ps 29-30	Acts 23:1-15	
JULY 22	Ps 31-32	Acts 23:16-35	
JULY 23	Ps 33-34	Acts 24	
JULY 24	Ps 35-36	Acts 25	
JULY 25	Ps 37-39	Acts 26	
JULY 26	Ps 40-42	Acts 27:1-26	
JULY 27	Ps 43-45	Acts 27:27-44	
JULY 28	Ps 46-48	Acts 28	
JULY 29	Ps 49-50	Rom 1	
JULY 30	Ps 51-53	Rom 2	
JULY 31	Ps 54-56	Rom 3	

AUGUST

DAY	OLD TESTAMEN T	NEW TESTAMENT	TICK (✔) After Reading For Each Day
AUGUST 1	Ps 57-59	Rom 4	
AUGUST 2	Ps 60-62	Rom 5	
AUGUST 3	Ps 63-65	Rom 6	
AUGUST 4	Ps 66-67	Rom 7	
AUGUST 5	Ps 68-69	Rom 8:1-21	
AUGUST 6	Ps 70-71	Rom 8:22-39	
AUGUST 7	Ps 72-73	Rom 9:1-15	
AUGUST 8	Ps 74-76	Rom 9:16-33	
AUGUST 9	Ps 77-78	Rom 10	
AUGUST 10	Ps 79-80	Rom 11:1-18	
AUGUST 11	Ps 81-83	Rom 11:19-36	
AUGUST 12	Ps 84-86	Rom 12	
AUGUST 13	Ps 87-88	Rom 13	
AUGUST 14	Ps 89-90	Rom 14	
AUGUST 15	Ps 91-93	Rom 15:1-13	
AUGUST 16	Ps 94-96	Rom 15:14-33	
AUGUST 17	Ps 97-99	Rom 16	
AUGUST 18	Ps 100-102	1Cor 1	
AUGUST 19	Ps 103-104	1Cor 2	
AUGUST 20	Ps 105-106	1Cor 3	
AUGUST 21	Ps 107-109	1Cor 4	
AUGUST 22	Ps 110-112	1Cor 5	
AUGUST 23	Ps 113-115	1Cor 6	
AUGUST 24	Ps 116-118	1Cor 7:1-19	
AUGUST 25	Ps 119:1-88	1Cor 7:20-40	
AUGUST 26	Ps 119:89-176	1Cor 8	
AUGUST 27	Ps 120-122	1Cor 9	
AUGUST 28	Ps 123-125	1Cor 10:1-18	
AUGUST 29	Ps 126-128	1Cor 10:19-33	
AUGUST 30	Ps 129-131	1Cor 11:1-16	
AUGUST 31	Ps 132-134	1Cor 11:17-34	

SEPTEMBER

DAY	OLD TESTAMEN T	NEW TESTAMENT	TICK (✔) After Reading For Each Day
SEPTEMBER 1	Ps 135-136	1Cor 12	
SEPTEMBER 2	Ps 137-139	1Cor 13	
SEPTEMBER 3	Ps 140-142	1Cor 14:1-20	
SEPTEMBER 4	Ps 143-145	1Cor 14:21-40	
SEPTEMBER 5	Ps 146-147	1Cor 15:1-28	
SEPTEMBER 6	Ps 148-150	1Cor 15:29-58	
SEPTEMBER 7	Prov 1-2	1Cor 16	
SEPTEMBER 8	Prov 3-5	2Cor 1	
SEPTEMBER 9	Prov 6-7	2Cor 2	
SEPTEMBER 10	Prov 8-9	2Cor 3	
SEPTEMBER 11	Prov 10-12	2Cor 4	
SEPTEMBER 12	Prov 13-15	2Cor 5	
SEPTEMBER 13	Prov 16-18	2Cor 6	
SEPTEMBER 14	Prov 19-21	2Cor 7	
SEPTEMBER 15	Prov 22-24	2Cor 8	
SEPTEMBER 16	Prov 25-26	2Cor 9	
SEPTEMBER 17	Prov 27-29	2Cor 10	
SEPTEMBER 18	Prov 30-31	2Cor 11:1-15	
SEPTEMBER 19	Ecc 1-3	2Cor 11:16-33	
SEPTEMBER 20	Ecc 4-6	2Cor 12	
SEPTEMBER 21	Ecc 7-9	2Cor 13	
SEPTEMBER 22	Ecc 10-12	Gal 1	
SEPTEMBER 23	Song 1-3	Gal 2	
SEPTEMBER 24	Song 4-5	Gal 3	
SEPTEMBER 25	Song 6-8	Gal 4	
SEPTEMBER 26	Is 1-2	Gal 5	
SEPTEMBER 27	Is 3-4	Gal 6	
SEPTEMBER 28	Is 5-6	Eph 1	
SEPTEMBER 29	Is 7-8	Eph 2	
SEPTEMBER 30	Is 9-10	Eph 3	

OCTOBER

DAY	OLD TESTAMENT	NEW TESTAMENT	TICK (✔) After Reading For Each Day
OCTOBER 1	Is 11-13	Eph 4	
OCTOBER 2	Is 14-16	Eph 5:1-16	
OCTOBER 3	Is 17-19	Eph 5:17-33	
OCTOBER 4	Is 20-22	Eph 6	
OCTOBER 5	Is 23-25	Phil 1	
OCTOBER 6	Is 26-27	Phil 2	
OCTOBER 7	Is 28-29	Phil 3	
OCTOBER 8	Is 30-31	Phil 4	
OCTOBER 9	Is 32-33	Col 1	
OCTOBER 10	Is 34-36	Col 2	
OCTOBER 11	Is 37-38	Col 3	
OCTOBER 12	Is 39-40	Col 4	
OCTOBER 13	Is 41-42	1Thess 1	
OCTOBER 14	Is 43-44	1Thess 2	
OCTOBER 15	Is 45-46	1Thess 3	
OCTOBER 16	Is 47-49	1Thess 4	
OCTOBER 17	Is 50-52	1Thess 5	
OCTOBER 18	Is 53-55	2Thess 1	
OCTOBER 19	Is 56-58	2Thess 2	
OCTOBER 20	Is 59-61	2Thess 3	
OCTOBER 21	Is 62-64	1Tim 1	
OCTOBER 22	Is 65-66	1Tim 2	
OCTOBER 23	Jer 1-2	1Tim 3	
OCTOBER 24	Jer 3-5	1Tim 4	
OCTOBER 25	Jer 6-8	1Tim 5	
OCTOBER 26	Jer 9-11	1Tim 6	
OCTOBER 27	Jer 12-14	2Tim 1	
OCTOBER 28	Jer 15-17	2Tim 2	
OCTOBER 29	Jer 18-19	2Tim 3	
OCTOBER 30	Jer 20-21	2Tim 4	
OCTOBER 31	Jer 22-23	Titus 1	

NOVEMBER

DAY	OLD TESTAMENT	NEW TESTAMENT	TICK (✔) After Reading For Each Day
NOVEMBER 1	Jer 24-26	Titus 2	
NOVEMBER 2	Jer 27-29	Titus 3	
NOVEMBER 3	Jer 30-31	Philemon	
NOVEMBER 4	Jer 32-33	Heb 1	
NOVEMBER 5	Jer 34-36	Heb 2	
NOVEMBER 6	Jer 37-39	Heb 3	
NOVEMBER 7	Jer 40-42	Heb 4	
NOVEMBER 8	Jer 43-45	Heb 5	
NOVEMBER 9	Jer 46-47	Heb 6	
NOVEMBER 10	Jer 48-49	Heb 7	
NOVEMBER 11	Jer 50	Heb 8	
NOVEMBER 12	Jer 51-52	Heb 9	
NOVEMBER 13	Lam 1-2	Heb 10:1-18	
NOVEMBER 14	Lam 3-5	Heb 10:19-39	
NOVEMBER 15	Ezek 1-2	Heb 11:1-19	
NOVEMBER 16	Ezek 3-4	Heb 11:20-40	
NOVEMBER 17	Ezek 5-7	Heb 12	
NOVEMBER 18	Ezek 8-10	Heb 13	
NOVEMBER 19	Ezek 11-13	James 1	
NOVEMBER 20	Ezek 14-15	James 2	
NOVEMBER 21	Ezek 16-17	James 3	
NOVEMBER 22	Ezek 18-19	James 4	
NOVEMBER 23	Ezek 20-21	James 5	
NOVEMBER 24	Ezek 22-23	1Pet 1	
NOVEMBER 25	Ezek 24-26	1Pet 2	
NOVEMBER 26	Ezek 27-29	1Pet 3	
NOVEMBER 27	Ezek 30-32	1Pet 4	
NOVEMBER 28	Ezek 33-34	1Pet 5	
NOVEMBER 29	Ezek 35-36	2Pet 1	
NOVEMBER 30	Ezek 37-39	2Pet 2	

DECEMBER

DAY	OLD TESTAMENT	NEW TESTAMENT	TICK (✔) After Reading For Each Day
DECEMBER 1	Ezek 40-41	2Pet 3	
DECEMBER 2	Ezek 42-44	1John 1	
DECEMBER 3	Ezek 45-46	1John 2	
DECEMBER 4	Ezek 47-48	1John 3	
DECEMBER 5	Dan 1-2	1John 4	
DECEMBER 6	Dan 3-4	1John 5	
DECEMBER 7	Dan 5-7	2John	
DECEMBER 8	Dan 8-10	3John	
DECEMBER 9	Dan 11-12	Jude	
DECEMBER 10	Hosea 1-4	Rev 1	
DECEMBER 11	Hosea 5-8	Rev 2	
DECEMBER 12	Hosea 9-11	Rev 3	
DECEMBER 13	Hosea 12-14	Rev 4	
DECEMBER 14	Joel	Rev 5	
DECEMBER 15	Amos 1-3	Rev 6	
DECEMBER 16	Amos 4-6	Rev 7	
DECEMBER 17	Amos 7-9	Rev 8	
DECEMBER 18	Obadiah	Rev 9	
DECEMBER 19	Jonah	Rev 10	
DECEMBER 20	Micah 1-3	Rev 11	
DECEMBER 21	Micah 4-5	Rev 12	
DECEMBER 22	Micah 6-7	Rev 13	
DECEMBER 23	Nahum	Rev 14	
DECEMBER 24	Habbakuk	Rev 15	
DECEMBER 25	Zephaniah	Rev 16	
DECEMBER 26	Haggai	Rev 17	
DECEMBER 27	Zech 1-4	Rev 18	
DECEMBER 28	Zech 5-8	Rev 19	
DECEMBER 29	Zech 9-12	Rev 20	
DECEMBER 30	Zech 13-14	Rev 21	
DECEMBER 31	Malachi	Rev 22	

SECTION THREE

FREQUENTLY ASKED QUESTIONS (FAQ) ON BIBLE READING

1. **What are the secrets of completing the Bible in one year?**

- Love for God and His Word
- Diligence, consistency, faithfulness, discipline
- Good time management
- Self-encouragement
- Holy living
- Prayer for the required grace and strength
- Always take note of where you stopped and make sure you continue from there without jumping
- This does not stop you from reading other chapters that you particularly need at a point in time, but make sure you don't stop or break off from your one-year Bible reading plan. Go back to where you stopped

2. **Why do I need to read the whole Bible?**

- The whole Bible is the inspired Word of God and contains truths that you need for life and godliness
- A Christian, who is spirit-filled and heaven-bound, must be an

authority on the whole Bible. The Bible is a book for all Christians, and not for Pastors and Ministers alone

- It is an embarrassment and a shame, when a Christian demonstrates ignorance of any part of the Bible
- A believer who does not know the whole Bible can easily be deceived and confused

3. **How do I handle passages that appear 'difficult or dry'?**

- Remind yourself that the whole Word of God is inspired and written for a purpose
- Tell yourself that there is no part of the Bible that is dry, useless or purposeless. You don't appear to need it now; but that 'dry' part has been useful for somebody in history, is quite helpful for some now, and you may need it one day.
- Read fast through such portions, but don't stop or abandon your Bible reading plan
- In preparing the One-Year Bible Reading Plan, we have ensured that you will read passages in

both Old and New Testament concurrently each day, to provide you with the spiritual nourishment that you need daily.

4. Is it advisable to mark my Bible with pen or marker?

- You need to mark your Bible with pen or marker, in order to pay particular attention to passages that powerfully strike you. This will also help you to memorize scriptures, refer to scriptures and know which portions of the Bible you have read
- God is not worried or upset with you that you mark and write in your Bible so you can know it more intimately.
- God is rather unhappy with you when your Bible is too clean because you don't read and study it aggressively

5. What is meditation, from the Christian perspective, and how do I meditate on the Word of God?

- Meditation from the Christian perspective means that you

think deeply on the Word of God. As you think, you want to understand its deepest meaning, how a particular passage compares with other passages, how it addresses life situations, and particularly the situations and experiences of your life, and how God would expect you to respond to the truth that He is now teaching you.

- Christian meditation is quite different and opposed to the demonic and occult practice of astral meditation, which requires that you blank your mind rather than exercise it actively. The blanking of the mind in occult meditation is so that demons may enter; unfortunately their preys don't seem to know this.

- For effective meditation, you need to love God and His Word, be spirit-filled, and know how to control your mind and thought, to achieve full focus and concentration. You also need a quiet place and a calm mind.

- You will also need to have and use different translations of the Bible, and other Bible study aids like Bible commentaries, Bible dictionaries etc.

6. **Why and how do I memorize passages of Scriptures?**

- Several Scriptures charge us to memorize the Word of God, hiding it in our hearts (Deut.6:6-9; Ps.119:11; Prov.4:20-22; Col.3:16). When you memorize a scripture, it becomes easier for you to know exactly what the scripture says, and live by such scriptures, through faith and obedience. It also becomes very handy in spiritual warfare.

- You memorize scriptures by opening it, reading it slowly, saying it to yourself and in your mind over and over again, and trying to quote it correctly after some time without opening the Bible.

- From my experience, most passages that I know by heart today are memorized by simply reading the passages over and over again, and meditating on them, because I got fascinated and excited by them.

- While meditation would require that you check several translations of the Bible, memorization is best done by using King James Version, or New King James Version.

7. What time is best time and place for reading my Bible?

- You can read your Bible anytime and anywhere. However, the environment must be quiet, with no distraction, while the time should be when you are fully awake, alert and can concentrate your mind.

- Night and morning hours appear to be the best, but you should also get used to reading your Bible every time, which is why you need to have the Bible on your phones, on your iPad, laptop and other electronic gadgets.

8. **What is revelation knowledge, and how do I receive revelation knowledge in God's Word?**

- Revelation knowledge is receiving a deep understanding and illumination of God's Word, through the help of the Holy Spirit, in a way you have never seen or understood it before. When it comes, it will also bring a great and deep joy and satisfaction into your spirit.

- To receive revelation knowledge, you must pray earnestly that the Holy Spirit will open your spiritual eyes of understanding, to behold wondrous things from His Word as the Bible says (Ps.119:18; Eph.1;15-18). You must be honest, be willing to receive the total truth of God's Word even when it chastises you. You must also be prompt to believe and obey the Word of God. The Holy Spirit will only give you new revelations when He sees what you have done with what he had earlier given you.

9. **What is the work of the Holy Spirit in knowing God's Word?**

- The Holy Spirit, the third Person of the Godhead, who has all the attributes of God, is the Author of the Bible. If you are a true believer, He came into you the day you gave your life to Christ, in a measure, though you need to be filled with Him and have Him in a fuller measure, through the wonderful experience of being baptized with the Holy Spirit, with the evidence of speaking in tongues. He alone is the one who, as Jesus says, will teach all truths and bring all truths we had known to our remembrance.

- You must seek to be filled and baptized with the Holy Spirit, with the initial evidence of speaking in tongues, if you have not had this experience.

10. What are the tips for applying, obeying and living by God's Word?

- You must be born again through faith in, and total submission to Christ, receiving Him as your personal Lord and Saviour. Until then, you will remain carnal, and the carnal man cannot understand or receive the things of the Spirit of God (Jn.3:6;Rom.8:5-8; I Cor.2:14)

- Know that the Word of God is the truth, the whole truth and nothing but the truth, and that it is given to you by God for your own good, so that you can be victorious in this life, live a holy life and make heaven.

- Choose and decide that you will obey and live by the Word of God all the time. Before you do anything, find out what the Bible says concerning His Word, and simply obey and live by that truth. If it is a promise, claim it with joy and confidence.

- Pray for the grace of God to empower you and give you moral strength to practise His Word, to find His yoke easy and His burden light.

- Put your faith in the finished work of Jesus Christ on the Cross of Calvary.

SECTION FOUR

COMMON PASSAGES THAT ALL CHRISTIANS MUST KNOW BY HEART

SN	THEME	PASSAGES TO KNOW BY HEART
1	On the Word of God	Jos.1:8; Ps.119:11, 18, 105, 130; Ps.1:1-3; Prov.4:20-22; Deut.6:6-9; II Tim.2:15; 3:16; Jn.6:63;
2	On Salvation through Jesus Christ	Is.53:5-6; Jn.3:3, 16-18, 36; Jn.14:6; Act 4:12; Act.16:31; Rom.3:23; 6:23; 8:1; Jn.6:37
3	Call unto repentance	Is.1:18; Ez.33:11; Act 17:30; Rev.3:20
4	Listing of sins	Mk.7:20-23; Rom.1:28-30; Gal.5:19-22; II Tim.3:1-5; Rev.21:8,27
5	Anyone in Christ is a New Creature	II Cor.5:17
6	The Fruit of the Spirit	Gal.5:22-23
7	God hates lukewarmness	Rev.3:14-16

8	On the Holy Spirit	Act 1:8; Rom.8:14, 16
9	On Holiness	Heb.12:14; I Pet.1:15-16; Rev.21:27
10	On Brevity of our Stay on earth and setting our earths on heaven	Ps.90:12; I Pet.2:11; Col.3:1-4; Jn.14:1-3; II Cor.4:16-18
11	On confession and forgiveness of sins	Ps.32:1-2; I Jn.1:8-9; Prov.28:19
12	On the Protection, Victory and Authority of the Believer	Ps.23; Ps.27:1-3; Ps.46:1-3; Ps.91; Ps.121; Is.54:10, 14, 17; Is.49:24-26; Lk.10:19; Matt.16:18; I Jn.4:4; I Jn.5:4
13	On answer to Prayer	Matt.7:7-9; 18;18-19; Jer.29:11,13; Mk.11:22-24; Jn.15:7; Jn.16:23-24
14	On Wisdom	Prov.4:7; Jas.1:5
15	On financial/material provisions	Deut.8:18; Phil.4:19
16	On giving	Lk.6:23

17	On God's Care for us	Matt.11:28-30; Phil.4:4-6; I Pet.5:7
18	On spiritual warfare	Ps.2; Ps.68:1-2; Eph.6:10-18; I Pet.5:8; Rev.12:11; II Cor.10:3-6
19	Prayer for the nation and intercession for others	II Chron.7;13-14; I Tim.2:1-4
20	Be Prepared for the consequences of your choice and action	Rev.22:10-12
21	The Mighty Name of Jesus	Is.9:6; Phil.2:9-11; Mk.16:17-18
22	God's Grace	Eph.2:8-9; Tit.2:11-12; Phil.4:13; II Cor.12:9
23	On Faith	Heb.11:1,6; Jas.1:6-8; Rom.10:17; Mk.9:23
24	Fear Not	Lk.12:32; Is.41:10; II Tim.1:7; Heb.13:5-6

25	Don't neglect Fellowship	Heb.10:25
26	The Lord is not slack concerning His Coming	II Pet.3:9
27	Iniquity shall abound	Matt.24:12-13
28	Few will be saved	Matt.7:13-14, 21-23; Lk.13:23-24; I Pet.4;17-18
29	Satan furious because his time is short	Rev.12:12
30	Love not the World	I Jn.2:15-17; Jas.4:4
31	The Great Commission	Matt.28:19-20; Mk.16:15-16
32	Signs of the End Time	Matthew chapter 24; Luke chapter 21
33	Sermon on the Mount	Matthew chapters 5, 6 & 7
34	The Ten	Ex.20:1-17

	Commandments	
35	Love God with all your heart	Deut.6:4-5
36	Our all-round blessings, after diligent obedience	Deut.28:1-14
37	Curses on disobedience	Deut.28:15-68
38	Train up Your Child	Prov.22:6
39	Conjugal responsibilities of husbands and wife	Eph.5:22-33; I Pet.3:1-7
40	God's exceedingly great and precious promises	II Pet.1:3-4
41	We are a chosen generation	I Pet.2:9
42	Call to worship God	Ps.100; Ps.103:1-7; Jn.4:23-24
43	Christ came so that we may have abundant life	Jn.10:10
44	The Gifts of the Holy Spirit	I Cor.12:7-10
45	The Five-Fold Ministry Gifts	Eph.4:11-12
46	The Supremacy of Love	I Cor.13
47	Rejoice in the Lord always	Phil.4:4; I Thes.5:16

48	Jesus gives us peace	Jn.14:27; Phil.4:6-7;
49	Pray without ceasing	Lk.18:1; I Thes.5:17
50	It is Finished	Jn.19:30; Jn.17:4

FELLOWSHIP WITH US

For you to run this race to the end victoriously, it important for you to locate a sound, Bible-believing, evangelical, Pentecostal church not far from where you live, where the issues of eternity are taken very seriously. Don't jump from church to church; be a committed, faithful and known member of the church to which you believe God has led you.

If you live around Okota in Lagos, please fellowship with us in the Foursquare Gospel Church, 43/49, Esuola Street, Off Ago Palace Way, Okota, Lagos.

Our Pastors are conscious that their responsibilities are to help and teach people to live victoriously and enjoy abundant life here on earth, but much more importantly, they teach, instruct, disciple, warn and help members to think daily of eternity and prepare themselves for heaven and to escape that terrible place called hell. They do all of these in the spirit of love and humility. We are conscious that we have responsibility for your soul, while we also strive to guard and keep ours.

Join us in church fellowship, and you will meet with God and experience a total transformation in your life.

THE FOURSQUARE GOSPEL CHURCH
OKOTA DISTRICT HEADQUARTERS
43/49, ESUOLA STREET
OFF AGO PALACE WAY
OKOTA, LAGOS

OUR DAYS OF FELLOWSHIP

- Sunday Worship: 8.00 - 11.15 am (with Sunday School Class in between)
- Tuesday Special Breakthrough Prayer: 7.00 - 9.00am
- Wednesday Bible Study: 6.00 – 8.00 pm
- Friday Prayer Meeting: 6.00 - 7.45 pm

OTHER BOOKS BY REV. DR. TOPE ONI

1. How to be Born Again
2. Now that You Are Born Again
3. How to be Baptized with the Holy Spirit
4. How to Make Heaven and Escape Hell
5. Hell is Far More Terrible than You Think
6. Making the Best of Your Critical Years
7. Lust-Free Christian Living
8. The Christian in a Corporate Environment
9. Effective Parenting

10. Comprehensive Bible Study Manual
11. Understanding & Appropriating the Grace of God
12. Hell is Far More Terrible than You Think
13. Confronting and Overcoming Nominalism in Today's Church
14. Whiter than Snow - Holiness, the Message of the Hour
15. The Truth of Grace; the Error of Hypergrace

To make your orders for any of the books, please call any of the following numbers – 07034138241, 08033085651, 08064967361

ABOUT THE BOOK

As one moves around in ministry, one is amazed and dumbfounded to realize that most Christians are largely ignorant of God's Word. Even common passages that used to be at the fingertips of the average Christian few decades ago are now completely strange to most believers today. The ignorance of God's Word by Christians accounts in large measure for the falling away of the church, the spiritual weakness and defeat of most believers, the emergence of the age of godfatherism and personality worship, and why many Christians fall victim of false doctrines and fallacious teachings.

The key problem is that many Christians don't know the value and power of the Bible and the fact that the whole of their lives depend upon it. This is the primary problem, followed by other secondary problems such as worldliness, busyness, indiscipline, poor time management, and frustration and discouragement when many people come across passages that appear dry or difficult.

This book will help you to have a better appreciation of the power of the Word of God and why it must occupy a central place in your life. It also addresses the Frequently Asked Questions on personal Bible Study. In addition, we present a One-Year Bible Reading Plan, to assist you in a systematic and comprehensive study of the Bible, by which you are able to read the Bible from cover to cover in one year. Finally, we outline basic, powerful and most useful passages that all serious Christians must know by heart. We trust that with discipline, prayer and determination, this book will turn your spiritual life around for good, in Jesus Name.

ABOUT THE AUTHOR

Rev. Dr. Tope Oni who holds a Ph.D degree in Sociology, is the District Overseer of Okota District and the Senior Pastor of The Foursquare Gospel Church, Okota, Lagos, Nigeria. Dr Oni was National Director of Youths for The Foursquare Gospel Church in Nigeria from 2004 to 2009 and member of the

National Board of the Board of Directors of the Foursquare Church in Nigeria, from 2014 to 2020. He is a Christian author of 15 books, to God's glory. He is a teacher of the Word, his teaching ministry having taken him to several tertiary institutions and several churches across denominations, within and outside Nigeria. His ministry focus includes: effective parenting; capacity building for teenagers, youths and corporate employees and entrepreneurs; passionate commitment to God's Word; seeking God in intimate personal relationship; and preparing for eternity. Besides being a Pastor, Dr Tope Oni has worked variously as University Lecturer, Banker and Management Consultant. He is married to Rev Mrs Bunmi Oni, his Associate Pastor. Their marriage is blessed with God-fearing children and grandchildren – all to God's glory!

.

www.ingramcontent.com/pod-product-compliance
Ingram Content Group UK Ltd.
Pitfield, Milton Keynes, MK11 3LW, UK
UKHW022007190726
13853UKWH00004B/1791